Five Long Years

Acknowledgements

When I was diagnosed with metastatic breast cancer, my daughters urged me to write my parents' story. When I was asked to join the Marshall writers group a short time later, I saw it as a sign. Thanks to the feedback and encouragement I received from the group, as well as from my husband and daughters, the story slowly emerged. Special thanks go to Joy Schaya and Bess Taylor who were instrumental in proofreading and publishing, Leny Nolten, my editor, for her many invaluable suggestions and Cyril van Dijk for his wonderful cover design.

IN HONOR OF

My father, Jacobus 1916-2001

My mother, Agatha 1923-2005

For my children and grandchildren

Five Long Years

By Maria N. Simpson

Cover Art by Cyril v. Dijk

Prologue

Spaarndam, Netherlands

August 31, 1927

Lena finished tying her little girl's apron and tucked a handful of peanuts into her pocket. "Now, go eat your nuts in the backyard and wait for us. Make sure you keep your Sunday dress and apron clean, you'll want to look pretty for the party!" "Yes, mama." Four-year-old Agatha slipped into her wooden shoes waiting by the back door and headed for the swing. She was feeling festive in her new dress and apron that mama had sewn for her. Today was a special day. Not only was it her birthday, but Queen Wilhelmina's as well. They were all going to the festivities in the village that afternoon. Carefully, she sat down on the swing, trying not to wrinkle her dress. As soon as she started to crack her peanuts, the chickens came clucking towards her in hopes of a stray morsel.

Pieter looked out of the kitchen window and saw little "Aggie" as he called her, surrounded by clucking and pecking chickens.

A smile formed on his otherwise stern face. She made quite a picture there with her white blond hair and dark brown eyes. He watched her share her peanuts with the chickens: "One for you, one for me." He didn't often get to spend a lot of time with his wife and daughters. Together with his brother and sisters he owned the Spaarndam village store. He got up every morning at 3 or 4 AM and headed into town to buy fresh produce for the business. When he came back, he had a quick breakfast and went to open the shop. Today, because of Queen's Day, the store was closed, and he was looking forward to spending the day with his family.

After lunch Pieter, Lena and their daughters Trudy and Agatha walked to the village square. Because it was her special day, Agatha rode on Papa's shoulders. She could barely sit still, she was so excited. On Queen's Day Spaarndam went all out: The Marching Band was playing.

The Dutch red, white and blue flags were cheerfully flapping in the breeze. There was orange bunting everywhere in honor of the Royal House of Orange birthday. There was a carousel and various booths offering a variety of activities and foods. Agatha was hoping for some "poffertjes". She loved the miniature pancakes, heaped on a plate and topped with butter and powdered sugar. As they approached, Aggie took in the colorful scene. All this for HER birthday? Papa and Mama and Trudy's birthdays had been nothing like this! Soon they were surrounded by friends and family. "There's our very own little Spaarndam queen."

The afternoon passed in a blur. A cousin took her on the carousel, an uncle bought her some spun sugar. She shared a plate of poffertjes with Trudy. There were activities for children: burlap sack hopping and three legged races. Agatha was too young to participate in some of them, but she loved to watch and cheer her older sister on.

Afterwards when they walked home, tired and happy, Agatha exclaimed, "My birthday is the best of all."

Chapter One

The Invasion

On the tenth of May 1940 Hitler's troops invaded the Netherlands. There was no declaration of war. As they had done during the First World War, the Netherlands had declared neutrality. In spite of this, in the middle of the night, German troops came across the eastern borders. Queen Wilhelmina would later say in her radio address to the nation, "Like a thief in the night the enemy has invaded our country."

On the fourteenth of May, Pieter was headed for Amsterdam early in the morning, in his model T Ford, to buy produce for his grocery store in Spaarndam. Along the way he was stopped by Dutch police. One of the policeman gestured for him to open his window and asked him to repeat the words "Scheveningen", "schrift" and "schat". Puzzled, Pieter did as he was asked. The policemen explained that there were reports that German soldiers in civilian clothing had been parachuted behind enemy lines. Germans pronounce the "SCH" combination of letters as "SH", whereas the Dutch pronunciation is "S" followed by a guttural "G", which most Germans are unable to imitate. Thus having established that Pieter was a bona fide Dutch citizen, they informed him that the city of Rotterdam was being bombed. His car and his services were needed to transport the wounded from the besieged city. They directed him to follow a truck full of Dutch soldiers. Thus enlisted, he joined a long line of cars and ambulances, all directed to follow the military transport. Pieter's mind was reeling: One moment he had been on his every day route to the produce market, the next moment he was part of a civilian army, drafted to transport the injured.

As they approached Rotterdam, Pieter could see smoke, or maybe dust rising from the city. Planes were flying over. He thought he heard fireworks, but realized they were bombs dropping and the firing of their defense trying to bring down the planes. Suddenly there was a deafening BOOM! In horror Pieter saw the truck with soldiers he had been following, explode. Mayhem broke out. The civilians were directed off the road to make way for ambulances and emergency personnel. From his position Pieter saw a lot of blood and body parts surrounding the exploded truck. He could only guess the truck had been bombed.

Pieter's emotions were in a turmoil. He felt a strong urge to flee home, to Spaarndam and his family. Away from this horror! He took a deep breath and forced himself to calm down. He had been assigned a task and he would see it through!

After some time, part of the road was cleared and the civilians were directed back on the road towards Rotterdam. In a daze Pieter followed directions. For three days he drove back and forth between Rotterdam and The Hague to take people out of the bombed city to the relative safety of The Hague. The residents of The

Hague were asked to take in refugees and aid workers. Pieter was offered a room by the kind family Vonders.

In the mean time on the home front Lena and her three daughters Trudy, Agatha and Dinah had no idea where their husband and father was. The country was in turmoil: War had broken out. They heard reports on the radio about the invasion: Heavy combat at the eastern borders and air raids on Rotterdam. All phone lines were down.

After three days Pieter was told his services and his Ford were no longer needed, and he could go home. Relieved he headed home to Spaarndam. He had been unable to get word to his family and knew that they had to be worried! The drive home seemed to take forever.

Finally he reached Spaarndam. As soon as he pulled up in front of the house, Lena and the girls came flying out of the front door. He got out of the car and spread his arms wide. All four flew into his embrace. Sobbing, Lena asked where he'd been. Between tears and kisses he explained in a few short words. During the next couple of days he gave a more detailed account of the events that had taken place during his absence.

Word of Pieter's return spread through the village. Spaarndam was a close knit community. Pieter, as their storekeeper was well known and liked. The whole town had been worried when he went missing.

After five days of heavy fighting, the Dutch had to capitulate. Five years of German occupation were to follow. In the beginning it didn't seem so bad. Life in Spaarndam resumed its normalcy: Children went to school, people went to work and farmers worked their farms. The Dutch government had been replaced by a German government, but in everyday life that didn't seem to make much of a difference, at first......!

A week or so after his homecoming, Pieter decided to take a trip to The Hague to return the clothes he had borrowed and to thank the kind family that had taken him in. Agatha, who was sixteen at the time, accompanied him. Mr. and Mrs. Vonders had a son Karel and a daughter Leny. Agatha and Leny hit it off right away on that first visit and having become fast friends, invitations were issued for Leny to come to Spaarndam and for Agatha to come and stay with them in The Hague. It was during one of Agatha's stays with Leny Vonders that Karel's friend Jacobus came over, saw Agatha and fell head over heels in love. And that is how my mother met my father.

Chapter two

Changes

Pieter was not doing well. Ever since his return home he had trouble sleeping and if he slept, he experienced horrible nightmares. Dr. Heusdens, the village doctor gave Pieter something to help him sleep. The traumatic things he had witnessed were giving Pieter trouble, he explained. After some time, things would get better, he promised.

In the meantime the effects of the German occupation became more and more noticeable. New rules and regulations were issued on a weekly basis: First of all the Dutch flag was banned. Displays of orange pennants or bunting in honor of the Dutch royal family were also strictly forbidden. They had to be turned in or destroyed. On public buildings where once the cheerful red, white and blue had flapped in the breeze, now the swastika was displayed. The next thing was the curfew; nobody was allowed to be out after dark. Everybody had to install black-out curtains. No light should be seen coming from any structure. In a time before navigation computers, pilots flew by recognizing landmarks such as rivers and towns. Thus, the whole country was completely blacked out to prevent British pilots from finding their way across the Netherlands to Germany. Pieter thought it was nonsense to install black-out curtains. During the summer in the Netherlands, daylight lasts from four or five AM to about ten PM. By the time summer was over and they would need artificial lights again, the German forces would be gone and everything would be back to normal, he predicted. How wrong he was!

Agatha's seventeenth birthday on the 31st of August signaled the end of summer. There was no Queen's Day celebration this year. The marching band did not play, there were no festivities, no flags or orange bunting in honor of Queen Wilhelmina's birthday.

The royal family and some Dutch government officials had been able to get away to England. Initially the Dutch population felt betrayed by this. They soon realized however, that this had been the right call. If they had stayed in the Netherlands, they would have been imprisoned and more than likely executed.

When September rolled around and the days were getting shorter, it became apparent they would need black-out curtains after all. This German occupation was not going to be over before winter.

The next new rule was that everybody needed to register for ration cards. Food, yard goods, clothing, yarn etc. were rationed. After that everyone had to turn in their radios. The occupying force did not want anybody to be able to listen to the British Broadcasting Corporation (BBC) or "Radio Orange" (RO) from England. (Named after the Dutch Royal Family the House of Orange). When the Dutch army capitulated, a small number had been able to get away to England where they worked closely together with the British forces. "Radio Orange" was the link between the occupied Netherlands and free Europe. R.O. transmitted coded messages for the underground resistance movement in regards to weapon droppings and enemy forces movements.

While the family was struggling to comply with the new rules, Pieter's health continued to decline. He was losing weight, coughed and complained about pain in his back. He tried to do his part at work, but soon he wasn't able anymore. When he started to cough up blood, Dr. Heusdens referred him to a lung specialist, who in turn referred him to a surgeon. Pieter was hospitalized and underwent exploratory surgery, where lung cancer was diagnosed. It had already spread too far. Nothing could be done. After a few days he was released from the hospital and sent home. As was common practice in those days, he was not told about the gravity of his condition. Lena and her daughters rejoiced in his homecoming, thinking he was going to recover from the surgery and be well again. Jacobus, who had already been to Spaardam to meet Agatha's family, came for another visit to wish Pieter a speedy recovery. He brought Agatha a beautiful gold and ruby necklace to commemorate the happy occasion. (As the oldest daughter, I inherited the necklace. It is very special to me and I wear it every day.)

While Lena and her daughters were dealing with Pieter's illness, all military personnel still in the Netherlands received a letter in the mail politely asking them to come and register. This was accompanied by a round-trip train ticket. Most complied with the request and did not return home. The round-trip ticket had been deliberately misleading. They were to spend five years in a prisoner of war camp. All people of Jewish faith (or blood) were required to register and had to wear the star of David on their outer clothing. Most complied. Who was to know that this would make them easy to find and be rounded up for relocation? Nobody knew about the death camps until after the war.

Besides the Jews, all young men had to register and were sent to work in ammunition factories in Germany. Most refused to go. They didn't want to manufacture ammo for the enemy, moreover these factories were frequently bombed by the British Air Force. Those that didn't go had to go into hiding and became so called "Onderduikers" (underdivers). Others had to provide for their families and couldn't afford to go into hiding. They went to Germany, worked in the factories for a wage and their families at home were able to keep their ration cards, which meant more rations for the loved ones left behind. (In hindsight, this enemy workforce was a big mistake the Germans made. The Dutch workers were in a unique position to sabotage the production. It took only one somewhat misshapen shell to jam up a machine gun....!)

Like so many others, Jacobus refused to go to Germany and thus had to go into hiding.

More and more people were directly or indirectly affected by change. Pieter's car was requisitioned by the occupying force. He hadn't been able to use it anymore because gasoline was impossible to come by. The town doctor was allowed to keep his car and when gasoline was no longer available some handyman built a contraption to burn woodchips and somehow the car hiccupped along on this energy source.

German soldiers routinely set up roadblocks. Any good form of transportation was stopped and cars, motorcycles or even bicycles were requisitioned. Fortunately, Agatha and her sisters had old, rusty bicycles. They were allowed to keep those.

Another huge change affecting thousands was the forced evacuation from all coastal regions. German forces expected an invasion from England, so all beaches were fortified. Where once children played in the sand and people swam in the ocean, the beaches were now transformed to minefields with concrete bunkers and rolls and rolls of barbed wire.

Jacobus's family had to leave their coastal home in Scheveningen and were able to rent a house in Holten in a rural area. The good part was that food was more plentiful in the middle of farm country. They were still able to get milk, eggs, potatoes and vegetables without rations. Jacobus moved in with his parents thinking that there in the countryside nobody would be looking for him. Initially he felt safe there until German soldiers started rounding up young men and Jewish families who were in hiding. He realized his family's residence was the first place they would be looking for him. He had to find another place to hide.

Trudy had gotten married and had moved to her husband's home in Haarlem. With the now empty bedroom, Lena offered Jacobus a place in her home. This was a very brave thing to do; anybody providing a hiding place for Jews or young men was punishable by law! It could mean prison, concentration camp or worse!

Jacobus gratefully accepted. He and his Irish Setter named King joined the household. Lena and Agatha were taken aback when Jacobus showed up with King. The invitation had not included the dog! Jacobus pleaded his case: He and King were inseparable and he alone would take care of the dog, he promised. With a sigh, Lena relented.

A cousin who was talented with hammer and saw made a hiding place in the attic. Jacobus was lucky though, due to its geographic location, Spaarndam was a relatively safe place to be. There was only one road in and out of the village along the dike next to the river. It could be seen from quite a distance. Once in a while German forces would conduct a "Razzia", a house-to-house search for contraband such as radios and weapons, but mostly "onderduikers", people in hiding. When German forces were seen on the dike road, the windmills were turned straight up; a sign of danger. This early warning gave Jacobus the chance to disappear to his secret hiding place until the danger had passed. For the rest of the time, he and King could go fishing in the river in an old leaky rowboat and at night after dark, he and a friend would row to a tiny island in the middle of the river where the friend had a radio hidden and listen to BBC and Radio Orange from England. Jacobus had wrapped his own brand-new radio in canvas and had buried it in his parents' yard in Holten in order to keep it out of German hands. The war news they heard from England was very different from the war propaganda the German forces put out. When they heard that the American and Canadian forces had joined the war effort, they were overjoyed. It was all soon going to be over, they predicted. Nobody knew it was going to be five long years.

(After the war my father dug up his radio in Holten and brought it home to Haarlem. We had it for years. I remember the dials always crunching with sand)

Chapter three

New normal?

Day-to-day life in Spaarndam and everywhere else in the Netherlands became more and more difficult. Everyday normal things that everybody had always taken for granted were no longer available: toothbrushes, toothpaste, soap and detergent. People had to be resourceful and come up with substitutes. They learned to brush their teeth with a piece of terrycloth over their fingertip and instead of toothpaste they used salt or baking soda. Cold, soapless sponge baths became the new normal. There was precious little energy and it was used for cooking or keeping warm, not for luxuries like a hot bath.

Lena's parents needed help. Opoe (grandma) and Opa (grandpa) needed to evacuate from their coastal home. Opa had gradually become more and more confused and demented. Opoe definitely needed help to look after him.

Lena saw no other option than to take her parents into her home.

Pieter's illness had progressed to the point where he was bedridden. He could no longer manage the stairs, so they had put a bed in the living room for him. Lena and Agatha took turns sleeping downstairs to look after his needs during the night. Lena gave Opa and Opoe the master bedroom. She and Agatha slept in turn downstairs or with Dinah.

It was a big adjustment, especially for Jacobus. He had grown up in a spacious house, with a cook, a maid and a nanny. Here they shared a small cottage with seven people. The work was never ending. Agatha had quit her job at a childcare center in the nearby town of Haarlem, to help her mother care for Pieter and her grandparents. Jacobus tried to make himself useful as much as possible and took on tasks Pieter had done in the past such as chopping wood and bicycle maintenance.

Rubber became unavailable. Jacobus became quite good at fixing leaky tires. He had learned to make some sort of glue with which he was able to put a patch on a leak. People were seen riding on garden hoses wrapped around the rims instead of tires or even on bare rims. The lack of rubber also meant no elastic to hold up your clothing (including underwear). Agatha crocheted drawstrings out of old yarn. The worst shortage of course was food. Bread had not been available since the beginning of the war. Holland had always imported wheat. In the western part of the Netherlands the main crops are tulips. That had always been a very successful export item. With the ports now controlled by the occupying force, import and export had come to a stand still. Thus, no wheat but plenty of tulip bulbs. They are an onion like bulb, but unfortunately don't taste a bit like onions. They filled hungry stomachs however, and people had no choice but to eat them.

One day King disappeared. The dog had gotten used to roaming around freely, and usually found his way home again. Jacobus went out looking for him, calling his name and whistling. King was not to be found. Jacobus was heartbroken. He and the dog had been best buddies for years. Agatha felt sorry for him and tried to console him, but secretly she and Lena were relieved the dog was gone. It had become harder and harder to find food for him. There simply were no table scraps!

The rations available on the ration cards became more and more meager. Jacobus, in hiding, did not have a ration card because he wasn't registered. Agatha was given an employee's name at the town hall who would give her a ration card. She had strict instructions to not contact this person in front of others and had to use a code word. Once a month she rode her bike to the Haarlem town hall and waited around the corner until all other personnel had left. Heart beating in her throat, she would go in, find the person and give the code word. She was given a ration card with a fictitious name on it and as fast as she could, she would leave the premises and head back to Spaarndam. Transactions like these were not uncommon; the so-called underground (or resistance) movement worked in many different ways, but if caught the punishments were severe!

Even with the ration card, the food they were able to buy was not enough. Fortunately, in Spaarndam, they were still able to supplement with potatoes, homegrown vegetables and fish from the river. At some point Agatha was offered a half goat, fully butchered for sale on the black market. She jumped at the chance. They hadn't had meat in a long time. Pleased with herself she brought home her purchase. Jacobus took one look at it and saw by the paws that it wasn't a goat, but a dog. He didn't say a word, he didn't eat any of it, but the rest of the family enjoyed their "goat".

For residents in the cities like Amsterdam, Rotterdam and Haarlem the food shortages were far worse. The rations (if at all available) were nowhere near enough to live on. People started foraging outside of town into the country side, going farm to farm, house to house, asking for food. On a daily basis the roads out of town were full of people pushing old prams or strollers, riding bikes with baskets fastened on them, anything in which they would be able to transport food if they were lucky enough to find some. Because of its proximity to Haarlem and Amsterdam,

Spaarndam saw its share of people on these so called "honger tochten" (hunger journeys). It was heartbreaking to turn people down, but Lena had a large family to feed. It was a struggle to find enough food to feed seven people. There was never any extra to give away. Agatha had a hard time turning hungry children away. One day when she was boiling a pot of potatoes (they were no longer peeled, throwing peels away was a waste) the doorbell rang and a little boy stood on the front stoop asking for food. Agatha didn't have the heart to send him away. She told him to wait, went into the kitchen and returned with a hot potato on a fork. "Blow on it" she said, "it's too hot, I just took it out of the boiling pot". The boy couldn't wait, though. He stuffed the potato in his mouth, no doubt blistering his mouth in doing so. He had simply been too hungry to wait.

All the food shortages, of course, caused weight loss. Most people's clothes hung around them like loose rags. There were no new clothes or even cloth to be had. Agatha had taken sewing courses at school. After she did some alterations on her own clothes, she did her mother's, grandmother's and sisters'.   Word got around in Spaarndam that Agatha was a whiz with the sewing machine. Soon people approached her and asked if she could do alterations for them. Not only did she do some major taking in, she also took old, faded clothes apart and sewed them back together with the faded side on the inside and the new looking inside on the outside. People offered her money, she refused. Money had become worthless. If you can't buy anything with it, what good is it? Coffee, tea, tobacco, yard goods, yarn, shoes and especially food had become the new currency. Agatha accepted potatoes and vegetables, basically anything edible and even old clothes as payment. Old clothes were taken apart and new ones were made. Old, moth eaten sweaters were unraveled.   The pieces painstakingly knotted together and a new sweater was knitted out of this old yarn. Sometimes the yarn was so thin and worn, she put two different colors together and got very creative with colors and patterns. In this way she was able to help others while her family benefitted from the potatoes, milk and eggs she received in payment.

Shoes were a whole other problem. There were none to be had. The German forces had requisitioned all leather for boots for their troops. The shoes that had still been in the stores at the beginning of the war were all sold out and shoe stores were closed. Fortunately, the Germans had no interest in the traditional Dutch wooden shoes. Produced in Holland, they were still freely available. Agatha's family, being country people had often worn them. Around the village everyone did. Whenever they went into town they wore leather shoes. Jacobus, having grown up in upper class homes in Rotterdam and The Hague, had never worn wooden shoes, but now he had no other choice. Agatha knitted warm, woolen socks (out of old yarn) and after a while and some practice he got used to them. Nothing keeps your feet warm and dry like a pair of wooden shoes with woolen socks inside. Every day was a new challenge to find food and to come up with substitutes for articles that were no longer available.

Chapter four

Honger Tocht

Pieter had lost his fight. Lena and her daughters moved around the house with red-rimmed eyes. Pieter's suffering in the past weeks had been intolerable. Dr. Heusdens had made daily visits. There was little he could do. He hadn't been able to procure the medications Pieter needed. Like food, gasoline and textiles, medicines, especially morphine, had all been requisitioned by the occupying forces to supply their ever needy armies. Lena and her daughters had steadily been at Pieter's bedside, watching him struggle for breath and moan in pain. As sad as they were, there was also a measure of relief to know that his suffering was finally over.

The funeral was a solemn affair. Pieter's brothers and friends carried his coffin from the house to the cemetery. Lena and her daughters walked behind the coffin. Both sides of the road were lined with villagers, silently watching the procession with hats in hand as a final goodbye. The town mayor gave a beautiful eulogy. Afterwards, the closest friends and relatives came back to the house for a cup of tea. The customary post-funeral coffee and sandwiches could not be offered.

That night Agatha was awakened out of a deep sleep. "Agatha, Agatha" her father's voice sounded. She jumped out of bed to see to his needs, only to realize that he was no longer there. Tears streaming down her face she got back into bed and crying silently, she eventually went back to sleep.

In the morning she found her mother at the kitchen table with a pot of tea. Lena poured her a cup and while she handed it to Agatha, she said, "I dreamed about your father last night, he was calling your name"

While Lena and her girls were coping with their grief, Opa's dementia was getting steadily worse. He had to be watched constantly to make sure he wouldn't get hurt or wander away. Eventually he became bedridden. The bed in the living room was once again occupied. He became incontinent. Without hot water, soap or detergent it was impossible to keep him clean. The smell of urine and feces permeated the living room. At one point Agatha caught him eating his feces. "It's good," he said "it's gingerbread". Retching, Agatha ran outside. After she had emptied her stomach, she went inside to once again help her mother clean up Opa. "This is not doable anymore, mama" she said. "This simply cannot go on." "I know" Lena answered, "There isn't another solution, we just have to do the best we can".

Even though in Spaarndam access to food was easier than in the cities, Lena's family was experiencing severe shortages. They had a lot of mouths to feed. The rations had become practically nonexistent and they were no longer able to purchase enough food to provide for their needs. Jacobus's family in Holten reported that there was still food to be had there. It was decided that Agatha and her younger sister Dinah would travel by bicycle to Holten. Jacobus objected: It was too dangerous for two young women to be on the road. He was outvoted. He could not go himself. As a young man he would have been picked up by German police the moment he had set foot outside of Spaarndam.

Agatha and Dinah set out at first light to join the hundreds of people on the roads on this hunger journey. It was a perilous trip. Several times they had to find cover in trenches along the shoulder because the road was being shot at from above. There were roadblocks and bombed-out bridges. After two days they arrived at Jacobus's parents' house. The following days they spent going from farm to farm in search of food. They were able to buy some eggs at one farm, some potatoes at another. Some farmers promised them some eggs the following day. It took them a week to gather all they would be able to carry on their bicycles. The traditional Dutch bike has a luggage rack in the back. Jacobus had raided other family members' bikes and mounted their luggage racks in the front of Agatha and Dinah's bikes. Thus loaded up front and back they set out for the trip home. Somewhere along the road they encountered a man who warned them that the Germans had set up a roadblock on the bridge ahead. They were requisitioning everybody's food and means of transportation. The man offered his help. He directed them to an empty soccer stadium where they could hide out under the bleachers. After dark he would come and get them, he promised. What to do? The man seemed trustworthy, so they took him up on his kind offer. They hid out under the bleachers in the soccer stadium. Would the man keep his promise? Sure enough, after dark, he showed up. He had rowed across the river and would row them across, but the boat was small and he would only be able to take one of the women and one bike, or the two bikes and come back for them. Agatha felt responsible for her little sister who was only thirteen at the time. She was not about to be separated from her and saw no other option than to send the two bikes with cargo. So, they waited again. In the dark the doubts came: Had it all been a ruse? Had there really been a roadblock on the bridge? Was the man as trustworthy as he seemed? Would they ever see their bikes with the precious cargo again? They had spent a good part of their family's savings on the food they had gathered. Hungry and cold they waited. After what seemed like an eternity the man showed up. He rowed them across the river and took them to a farmhouse. The farmer's wife greeted them warmly. "You must be hungry and tired, I have soup and bread for you, but you probably want to see your bikes. I'll show them to you. They are safely locked away." Their relief was vast. After a bowl of soup and some bread they were given a place to sleep in the hayloft. There were more travelers there, all grateful for the helping hands extended to them. In the morning they were all given a glass of milk and another slice of course, homemade rye bread before setting out. They reached home that night. The last stretch was after curfew (dark) which was strictly forbidden. The family was already in bed. Jacobus, who hadn't been able to sleep much while they were gone, heard them and came to help them with the bicycles. Shaking with exhaustion they got off their bikes. Jacobus sent them to bed while he unloaded the bikes and parked them in the shed. They were home, safe and sound.

The next day they were told that during their absence their grandfather had died. Tears filled Agatha's eyes.

She had to admit to herself: they were tears of relief. This horrible trip was over and so was the impossible task of caring for Opa. Would things finally get a little easier? She felt a glimmer of hope.

Agatha undertook two more trips to Holten to get food. Both times she went with a friend. The responsibility for her little sister had been too great!

Chapter five

A new baby

Trudy and her husband Cornelius were expecting their first baby and they needed help. Cornelius ran his family's grocery store and after they got married, Trudy had taken over the administration. With the present rationing this was a cumbersome job. All outgoing goods had to agree with the ration coupons they had received from their customers. Now that Trudy was big and pregnant she was staying in their apartment above the store to prepare for her baby's arrival. She asked if Agatha could come and help her with the baby. She herself had no knowledge of baby and childcare. Agatha had worked in a childcare center and had taken courses in school. Cornelius needed help in the store. Somebody had to take over Trudy's administrative duties. He also needed help guarding the store. The food shortages had made people desperate. There had been several occasions of attempted burglaries. He asked if Jacobus could come and help. He sent an employee with a "bakfiets" (a Dutch cargo bike, the carrier ahead of the handlebars) to pick up Jacobus from Spaarndam. Hidden in an old rug and furniture stacked around him, he was transported from Spaarndam to Haarlem. They planned to stay for several months. Agatha was to help take care of the baby and the household. Jacobus would make himself useful behind the scenes, out of sight of customers doing admin work and take his turns standing guard. There were several young men, all hiding from the Germans, helping guard the store. It was an arrangement that worked for everyone. Cornelius had help, the young men had a relatively safe place to stay and were fed on a daily basis.

Jacobus was puzzled. Several times he had come up short with rationing coupons. No matter how carefully he counted, there was more food sold than the coupons they had taken in. Cornelius couldn't come up with an explanation either. Every night the accounts were carefully counted and most nights they agreed. Once or twice a week they came up short. There were severe punishments for selling or giving away food without the necessary rationing coupons. Did one of his employees do this? He decided to keep his eyes and ears open. When it happened again he noticed that every time they came up short, Mrs. Jansen had been in. She always asked if she could use the restroom. Cornelius decided someone needed to spy on her. He drilled a peephole in the ceiling of the restroom and Trudy in the upstairs apartment had to spy on Mrs. Jansen to see what she was doing. Trudy protested: with her big pregnant belly she could not be expected to lay on the floor to peek down the peephole. The task fell to Agatha. Sure enough, on her way to the restroom Mrs. Jansen stepped into the unmanned office, grabbed a handful of coupons and in the restroom she stuffed them in her underwear. Mrs. Jansen who had been a regular and pleasant customer for years had to be banned from the store. Even the most trustworthy people would resort to thievery just to fill an empty stomach.

One day Cornelius noticed some snickering among his employees. There seemed to be a lot of need for the restroom. He decided to investigate. On the bathroom wall was the following poem:

Ons land is als dit cabinet

Eerst was het vrij, nu is het bezet.

Het is hier als in de Nederlanden

Geen winst doch enkel offeranden

Alles komt hier zoals in ons land

Onder zware druk tot stand.

Ook hier wacht men in stille wijding

Op het moment van de bevrijding

Maar onder het zuchten dat wij horen

Wordt weer een schone hoop geboren

Ten slotte geldt voor allebei

Heel spoedig zijt gij weder vrij

Hoe opgelucht zult gij u voelen

Als ge al het vuil weer weg ziet spoelen

Freely translated it goes something like this:

Our land is like this restroom

First it was free, now it is occupied

It is here as in the Netherlands

No gains, but only losses

Like in our country

Everything here happens under heavy pressure

Here too one waits in silent dedication

For the moment of the liberation

How relieved you will feel

When you'll see all that waste flushed away

He couldn't help but laugh. He didn't ask who had written it on the wall. He just ordered it washed away and painted over. It was simply too dangerous to leave it there. Customers sometimes used the restroom and if word got out, it could cause a lot of trouble. For a brief time the poem had lifted their spirits. After the war they found out that the poem had been on bathroom walls all over the country. The poet, of course, is unknown.

Trudy gave birth to a healthy baby boy. They named him Pieter after his deceased grandfather. Agatha instantly fell in love with her little nephew. She enjoyed helping to take care of him. She loved being at her sister's. They had settled into a comfortable routine. She helped with the housework, the cooking and the baby. Jacobus helped in the store. Food was more plentiful than at home and life seemed a little easier here.

Then one day a Dutch policeman who worked closely with the German authorities (who was considered a traitor by many) passed on the information that the Germans had been made aware of the young men hiding out in the store and warehouse. As a thank-you he received some extra rations. Jacobus was transported back to Spaarndam in the same way he had come. Agatha decided her sister and nephew didn't need her anymore and also moved back to Spaarndam.

Chapter Six

Razzia

Life resumed with the daily struggle to find food and fuel for heat and cooking. Many people rigged up a bicycle in the living room. Family members would take turns pedaling to turn the wheel in order for the dynamo to produce electricity to power the headlight, thus providing some much needed light for darning socks, knitting or mending. In winter, in Holland, daylight doesn't come until about 9AM and by 3PM it starts getting dark again. Those were long, dark and cold evenings. Most of the time they would just go to bed early to stay warm and save on fuel for heating.

One such night when everyone had gone to bed early, they woke up from a commotion outside. They heard loud banging on doors and German commands: "Aufmachen Razzia!" It was a house-to-house search the Germans conducted from time to time. The family knew the drill: They had practiced this. Agatha and her little sister shared a double bed. During a Razzia she would crawl into Jacobus's bed while he went up to the attic to his hiding place. His clothes were always in Lena's wardrobe among Pieter's things. This way there was no vacated bed (still warm) and no man's clothing found in this all female household. They barely had enough time to accomplish all this when there was banging on their front door. Lena opened the door. German soldiers, accompanied by a Dutch policeman came in and searched the house. Everyone had to get out of bed and was ordered to the living room. Wrapped in robes and blankets, shivering in the cold and with fear they did as they were told. Upon entering the living room, Opoe saw the one thing they had overlooked: Jacobus's tobacco pot. She quickly pushed it under a chair, sat down on the chair and spread her blanket around it. One by one the family members were questioned. The Dutch policeman translated, "Did they have contraband such as weapons or a radio? Were they hiding Jewish or other wanted persons (such as young men)?" Of course, the women all demurely answered, "No, sir, of course not, sir." When

Opoe was questioned, she answered, "I don't understand German." The Dutch policeman repeated his question, again the same answer, "I don't understand German." The rest of the women held their breath: What would they do with her, what would happen now? After several attempts to communicate with grandma the policeman shrugged his shoulders and told the German soldiers that the woman was old and demented and they would not be able to get a sensible word out of her. Meanwhile, the German soldiers had searched the house. The men's clothes in Lena's wardrobe were explained as her deceased husband's. Finally, after what seemed like an eternity, they left the house. The women didn't dare to get Jacobus out of his hiding place until they were sure the soldiers had left Spaarndam. Frozen to the bone, he was put in a warm bed and given hot tea to thaw out. There hadn't been time to put on clothes or a robe. He had lain for hours on the attic, directly under the roof in just a pair of worn, thin cotton pajamas.

In the morning when everyone had stopped shaking and everything had calmed down, Lena asked her mother why she had told the policeman she couldn't understand German, when clearly he had spoken Dutch. "I knew that," she said, "but I didn't know what else to say."

One night, after curfew, there was a soft knocking on the window. Who could that be? Nobody was allowed out after dark. Jacobus quickly went up to the attic, while Agatha went slowly down the hall, closing doors behind her, so no light would spill out when she opened the front door. In the dark, cold and hungry, was a distant cousin of hers. Agatha brought him into the living room where there was a meager fire and gave Jacobus the "all-clear". Derek, a young man like Jacobus, had been in hiding but could no longer stay at the address where he had been and asked if he could stay there for a while. What to do? The cottage was already crowded and another mouth to feed when food was already scarce was not easy to do, but they decided they couldn't turn him out into the cold night, so Lena told him he could stay for a little while, while he looked for another place. Jacobus offered to share his room. He went outside with Derek to get his things and put his bike in the shed. He marveled at

Derek's brand-new bicycle. Nobody had nice bicycles anymore. They had all been requisitioned by the Germans. Everybody rode old, rusty bikes, often without tires. Derek's bike had good, rubber tires. When back in the living room, Derek told the tale of his new bicycle. He had been stopped at a roadblock the Germans had set up on a bridge. They took his bike from him and ordered him to walk on. Derek spotted a row of bicycles leaning against the railing of the bridge, presumably taken from previous unlucky travelers. He glanced around: the soldiers were occupied with other people coming onto the bridge. He grabbed his chance. He took the nicest looking bike of the bunch and rode off as quickly as he could. There were no commands to stop or shots fired. Apparently the soldiers hadn't seen him. The young people laughed at his daring and defiance but Lena and her mother exchanged a worried glance. Would Derek fit into their household? They believed in keeping a low profile.

Chapter seven

The arrest

The first couple of days went well. Derek helped around the house with chores, but soon became restless and frustrated with being confined in a small space with so many people. When one night, out of boredom, he was playing with matches and started a fire in an ashtray, thereby singeing Dinah's hair, Lena told him he had to find another place to stay. He gathered his few belongings and left in a huff.

Unbeknownst to the family, he went to the German authorities and turned himself in. Out of spite, he turned Jacobus in as well. In the middle of the night the Gestapo came for him. There was no advance warning, no time to get away. They busted the door open, lifted him from his bed and hauled him away in handcuffs.

The days following the arrest were an emotional roller coaster. What happened to Jacobus? Was he being tortured? Would he be released after questioning? Would the Gestapo come back and arrest Lena, who as head of the household had provided a hiding place? There was so much fear and uncertainty, they didn't know what to do. Cornelius put together a food basket from his store and bribed the same Dutch policeman who had given him information before, to look into the matter. Food was the only currency that had any value. Even though it was against the rules and at great danger to himself, the policeman couldn't resist the temptation of some extra rations. A couple of days later he reported back: Jacobus had been taken to the Prisoner of War camp in Amersfoort. The news came as a relief. It had all been a big mistake. Jacobus had never been in the Military. All they had to do was come up with proof of this fact and surely he would be released. Agatha searched through Jacobus's personal effects and lo and behold she found the official notification that he had been rejected for military service due to the unfavorable outcome of his physical. She decided to go to Amersfoort and see to the matter herself. The weather was dismal; cold and rainy. Like everybody else, Agatha wore wooden shoes around Spaarndam, but she felt this was not an option when she wanted to make a good impression on the German authorities. She had one pair of decent leather shoes, purchased just after the beginning of the war, when Jacobus had had the foresight to realize there weren't going to be any leather shoes available soon. She had been saving them for her wedding day. In her best clothes and her wedding shoes she got on the train in Haarlem, armed with Jacobus's paperwork and enough money and food rations for a few days. This was most of the family's rations, but they had assured her they'd manage without and procure food somehow. When she reached Amersfoort, she immediately went to the gate of the POW camp and stated her business. The guards told her to come back the next day. The person she needed to speak to had already left for the day. She found some lodgings; a miserable little room with a narrow bed and a threadbare blanket, nowhere near enough to keep warm.

She spent a cold, sleepless night. When she heard German soldiers shouting commands, she carefully peeked through a slit in the curtains: Hundreds of prisoners, chained together were herded through the streets of Amersfoort towards the train station. Shuddering with fear and cold she returned to bed. The following morning the landlady provided a meager breakfast against payment of a large amount of money as well as a heap of rations. She had to eat to keep up her strength, she had no other option than to pay the exorbitant price. Dressed in her best clothes and shoes, she presented herself at the camp again. She was directed to a secretary who put her name on a list and was told to wait. She waited all day to no avail. She never did get to speak to the man in charge. The secretary took pity on her and suggested maybe she should go see Sister Nefkens, a nurse in charge of the camp clinic.

After another miserable, cold, sleepless night, listening to the sounds of another prisoner transport, fear clutched at her heart. Was Jacobus on a transport like this? The next morning she found Sister Nefkens's office. The nurse listened to Agatha's story and seemed sympathetic to her plight. She told Agatha there wasn't a whole lot she could do but she checked the lists of prisoner transports of the last few days and also of the next few days and Jacobus's name wasn't on any of them. She promised Agatha she would get Jacobus's paperwork to the proper authorities. Hopefully, this would result in a speedy release. She wasn't able to make promises though. The following morning, bright and early Agatha was at the gate. She had checked out of her lodging and was prepared to wait for Jacobus's release. She had brought clothes and a hat for him to wear on the way home. When the Gestapo had hauled him off he had only worn pajamas. After waiting at the gate from sunup to sundown for three days, she ran out of money and food rations. There was no other option than to buy a train ticket with the last of her money and return home.

Chapter eight

Jacobus

Dazed and shivering, cold to his bones in his thin pajamas, wrists shackled behind his back, Jacobus was being whisked away from Spaarndam and the people he'd come to care for. He kept seeing their faces in the pitch dark; the looks of horror and fear and the tears on Agatha's cheeks. "It'll be all right," he had managed to shout at her on his way out of the door. He doubted she had believed him. He didn't really believe it himself. He was realistic enough to know that a good outcome was unlikely. So many people rounded up by the Gestapo were never heard of or seen again. No one knew what had happened to them. They had just simply disappeared.....! The military vehicle he was being transported in came to a halt. By the dim light he recognized the Gestapo headquarters in Haarlem. Nothing good happened there....! He was pulled out of the vehicle and roughly pushed into the building, into what looked like an interrogation room. After what seemed like an eternity an officer came in and started questioning him. After asking for his name and birthdate, he wanted to know why Jacobus was in Spaarndam. Not wanting to incriminate Agatha's family who had provided a hiding place, he told them he had just come for a short visit. The officer clearly didn't buy it. "We have received information that you have been living there for quite some time and have not registered with the authorities." This was true, what could he say? But who had provided that information? All the time he had been in Spaarndam, none of the villagers had ratted him out. Why now? Suddenly it became clear: the only "new" person around had been Derek, the cousin. They should have known….!

After hours of interrogation the officer announced he would be transported to Amersfoort. Every Dutchman knew there was a concentration camp in Amersfoort. It had a horrible reputation, but no one knew for sure what happened there and how the inmates were treated.

The next day he was thrown into a truck, together with other prisoners. On the way to the camp no-one dared to say a word. The German guards forbade any form of communication. When they got there, some of the prisoners were unloaded, others stayed on the truck to be taken to a different location, Jacobus assumed. He was processed and assigned a bunk. One of his new bunkmates tried to put him at ease: "Don't worry, it is not as bad as it seems. As prisoners of war they have to treat us according to the Geneva Convention." The man was eager for news from the outside world. When Jacobus reported on the shortages on the outside; food, clothing and fuel for cooking or heating, the man told him to count his blessings, although the rations were meager, they were provided with food. They even received Red Cross packages with food, toiletries and sometimes even cigarettes. Jacobus confided that he had never been inducted into the military and it had all been a mistake. The man put his finger on his lips and made a shushing sound: "I wouldn't share that information with anyone if I were you." Puzzled Jacobus settled into camp life. There was a set schedule for everything; the day started being awoken by a loud whistle and a guard shouting, "Aufstehen, Fruehsport!" (get up, morning sport). They were to assemble and run on a track, several times around the compound. The track was covered in cinders, burned out coal, which was quite common in Holland at the time. Coal was the main source of heat well into the sixties. The cinders were commonly used to pave garden paths and walking trails through parks. A couple of guards found perverse pleasure in sticking the barrel of their rifle between a running prisoner's legs. They hooted and laughed when a prisoner fell and had cinders imbedded in his hands and knees.

After a couple of weeks Jacobus had settled in. He had found out which guards to stay away from and had learned to avoid attracting attention to himself. Things could be worse, he supposed.

One day he was summoned to the camp commander. "We have received information that you have never been in the military." The man had a form letter in his hand that Jacobus recognized. How had he gotten a hold of that? That had been safely hidden with his personal effects. Suddenly, hope flared up. Agatha! She had found a way to get him out of here. It was short lived. "We are transferring you to the concentration camp," the commander said.

Chapter nine

Agatha

Back in Spaarndam life went on with the day-to-day drudgery of trying to provide food and fuel to cook it. Spring came and with the weather warming up came the promise of home grown vegetables and potatoes. The women had dug up the back yard and where once flowers, shrubbery and grass grew, they planted rows of vegetables and potatoes.

Agatha kept hoping to hear from Jacobus. She had sent a message through the Red Cross, but she had received no answer or confirmation that he had received it. She had sent a letter to Jacobus's parents to let them know about the arrest, but had not received a response. The mail was unreliable. They might not have received it. There was no way to know. Phone lines were down. The unreliable mail was the only way to stay in touch.

In June rumors were whispered among the villagers in Spaarndam. Have you heard? The Allies have invaded Normandy, France. There was no way of knowing how true these rumors were. No-one dared to ask where the information came from. If someone had a radio and listened to the BBC or Radio Orange from England, it was better not to know. Since Jacobus wasn't there anymore to row out to the island in the river to listen to the radio he had hidden there, they had no means to confirm the rumors. None of the women knew how to work the radio and with the lack of food they didn't have the energy to row out there. But the rumors kept circulating; the allies were supposed to be pushing north. Hope flared; soon the Allied tanks will be rolling in and the Germans will retreat. "Before you know it, it'll be all over, you'll see," some of the more optimistic villagers said. According to German propaganda, the Allied Forces had made an unsuccessful attempt to breach the heavily guarded beaches of Normandy, but they preferred to believe the more positive news that the Allied Forces were pushing north. They clung to hope and waited.........Nothing happened. It wasn't until after the war that they learned the offensive had stalled south of the river Rhine. The southern part of the Netherlands was liberated. The people north of the river were to face the harshest, most difficult conditions yet. The winter of 1944/1945 has gone down in history as the "honger winter" (hunger winter). With temperatures far below average and no fuel to keep warm, people were desperate. In desperation they went out after dark, despite curfew, and sawed down trees, fences, park benches, anything that would burn. When no more wood could be found outside, they burned bedroom doors, banisters, doorframes, anything to keep from freezing. On the advice of the Dutch government in England, railroad workers went on strike to hamper the German supply lines to their fronts in Russia and the south of the Netherlands. In retaliation, the Germans cut off the already meager rations to the Dutch population. Lena's family survived with homegrown potatoes, eggs from their chickens, some fish from the river. In cities such as Amsterdam, Rotterdam, The Hague, Leyden and Haarlem, people died of starvation. After the war Agatha received a significant inheritance from an aunt and uncle in Leyden. Even though they'd had enough money, they had been unable to obtain food and died of hunger. The ground was too frozen to bury the dead. There was no fuel for cremation, no wood for coffins. The corpses were piled up until the weather warmed and the ground softened so they could be buried. Would this war never end?

Chapter ten

Jacobus

"The concentration camp", Jacobus knew was different from the POW camp, but he had no way of knowing in what way. He soon found out. Upon his arrival, he was given a prison suit and directed to put it on. The suit had a bullet hole on the left side of the chest area, surrounded by a large stain of dried blood. On the inside was dried-in feces. It was evident that the previous wearer of the suit had been shot and in his fear his bowels had released. When Jacobus wanted to point this out to the guard he was clobbered in the head with a rifle butt and commanded in no uncertain terms to strip and put on the suit. There was no other option than to obey......! Afterwards, he was questioned by several different officers. Where did he come from, where did he grow up? They seemed especially interested in his ancestry. Jacobus, with pitch black curly hair, bright blue eyes and a large nose, looked very Jewish, as did his father. There was nothing in his birth or family records though, that suggested he had any Jewish heritage. After several hours of questioning, he was assigned a bunk house, but first his hair had to be shaven off, to control lice, he was told. He soon found that was to no avail. The barracks he was assigned to was a dismal place. All the men were bald, had the same prison suits on and looked pale, tired and emaciated. There were no individual bunks. There was just one continuing bunk along the wall, where all the men piled up and tried to sleep. Once a day they received a bowl of watery slop, which everybody ate immediately. There was no saving a part for later. It would just get stolen. The only beings getting enough to eat were the lice. They were everywhere. In the beginning Jacobus would pick them off and kill them, but there were just too many of them. He watched as lice latched themselves onto him and sucked themselves full of blood.

Every morning was role call. Some men were told to step aside and were taken away. Some came back after being interrogated, others were never seen again. Every morning everyone had the same fear: "Will it be me today?". Every couple of days they were taken to "work" in the Rose Garden. Everyone dreaded Rose Garden duty. It consisted mainly of standing at attention for extended periods of time. Suffering from malnutrition and dysentery, it was extremely difficult and only shear willpower and fear kept them standing. The unfortunate man whose body gave out and collapsed, would be brutally beaten until he was back on his feet. Some men handled the constant threat better than others. The ones that suffered the most under this psychological warfare were married men with families. Jacobus was glad he'd been adamant about not getting married and starting a family. Agatha and he had talked about it many times. Both knew the circumstances were just too grim. He knew if he did not make it out, Agatha would be OK and would move on.

One day when Jacobus was feeling especially weak because he had a bad case of dysentery, they received the dreaded Rose Garden orders. He knew he would not be able to keep standing. As his group was being escorted into the Rose Garden, another group was escorted out. The guards exchanged a few words and Jacobus grabbed his chance. He left his group and joined the group that was leaving. His heart hammered loudly in his chest. Would he get away with it? He feared the punishment that would await him if he was found out, but he also knew what awaited him if he collapsed while standing at attention. There was no shouting, no shots rang out. Apparently the guards had not noticed. If his fellow prisoners saw, they did not say anything. He was able to repeat this maneuver several times. He knew he had to save his strength.

Days turned into weeks and weeks turned into months. His senses dulled, he didn't care anymore. Several times he was picked out of role call line for questioning. Always the same questions about his heritage. After hours of interrogation he was always sent back to the barracks. Others were not so lucky. After the war we learned that Amersfoort concentration camp was a so-called "Durchgangslager", a sorting camp where prisoners from the Netherlands were initially put. There it was decided whether they would be transported to an extermination camp in Germany or Poland. There were also destinations such as ammunitions factories, grave digging crews or work camps. Every night large numbers of prisoners were taken to the train station and put on trains for various destinations.

Chapter Eleven

Agatha

It was the twelfth of February 1945, when Agatha was on her way home from Haarlem after visiting with Trudy and little Pieter. She was in a good mood. She had hit it lucky today. Cornelius had given her a bag full of oats. Normally, he wasn't able to help much with extra food. Even though he owned a grocery store, everything had to be accounted for with the rations he received from his customers. This time a shipment of oats had gotten wet during transport and could not be saved. He handed out bags of wet oats to family and friends. Agatha just happened to be there and caught a lucky break. She was pedaling as fast as she could. It was very cold and she needed to get home to Spaarndam before curfew at dusk. She needed to cook the oats as soon as she got home to keep them from molding. She planned to take her mother's largest soup pot, or would she need two? What was she going to use for fuel? Thus deep in thought she was headed for the Jan Gijzen bridge where she would cross the canal, the shortest and her usual route home. Suddenly she noticed a lot of activity at the bridge. Several cars and trucks drove up to the bridge. She recognized German soldiers and the SS. What were they doing? Were they setting up a roadblock on the bridge? No way was she giving up her oats. Not sure what to do, she got off her bike, looking for a place to hide. The house she was in front of had a small entry way. She placed her bike behind a hedge, out of sight, and hid in the entry way. Either the occupants were not at home or too scared to open the door. She peeked around the corner. She watched the soldiers drag eight handcuffed people out of the truck. Prisoners? What was going on? The people were lined up on the bridge. The SS Officers rounded up passers-by and bystanders. They were told to stand there and watch.....The soldiers received the command to aim. At the next command a salvo of shots rang out. Agatha stifled a scream. She closed her eyes in horror. She did NOT just witness an execution! She was frozen to the ground. All of a sudden she knew she had to get out of there. Away from this bridge, away from this tragedy she had just witnessed. All she knew was that she needed to get back to Spaarndam.

It was way after dark and curfew when she got home. Fortunately, she knew the dike road along the river like the back of her hand. It was pitch dark and she could not turn her lights on. Being out after curfew was strictly forbidden and could land her in jail or worse. Lena, Opoe and Dinah were relieved to see her. They had gotten very worried when curfew came and Agatha was not home. They helped her cook the oats and were happy about the unexpected extra food. They noticed, though that something was wrong. Agatha was not her usual self. When asked questions about Trudy, Cornelius and little Pieter, she wouldn't answer. Opoe asked what was wrong and what had made her come home so late. She just shrugged her shoulders and didn't answer.

Within a couple of days, first rumors, then reliable reports reached Spaarndam. Eight prisoners, suspected of being involved in the Dutch resistance, were randomly selected and executed on the Jan Gijzen bridge in retaliation of two German Officers that had been attacked on the same bridge the previous day. When Lena heard the report, she asked her daughter. Agatha could only nod. She did not speak of what she had witnessed until many, many years later.

Spring was in the air. After a long, hard winter temperatures were rising, and with that came the promise of fresh food from the garden. They were hoping this would help against the seeping skin sores which they had developed. Dr. Heusdens had been consulted. He had told them, the problem was wide spread and caused by malnutrition. At least there wasn't the constant challenge of finding fuel to keep from freezing. Again rumors started to circulate through Spaarndam. Have you heard? There is talk of a peace treaty. Maybe it'll soon be over. Agatha was skeptical. After getting her hopes up in the past, only to be disappointed, she didn't dare hope anymore. She just carried on with the daily grindstone of survival. Her mother had never fully recovered from the loss of her husband.   The challenges of coping with shortages during wartime were too much for her. Gradually the function of head of household had shifted to Agatha. She had taken on the responsibility of securing enough food to feed her grandmother, mother and sister. She sewed, mended and altered old clothes, ripped bedsheets etc., all in exchange for food.   Rumors of a peace treaty left her unmoved.   "I'll believe it when I see it", she thought.

Chapter twelve

Jacobus

Even in the camp rumors of a peace treaty started to circulate. Nobody knew where they originated. The hopeful news spread among the prisoners. Some got their hopes up, others were skeptical. Similar rumors had been spread before and things had not changed. They were still here. During daily role call, men were picked out of the line and herded away. They did not come back. Nobody knew what had happened to them. One morning Jacobus's name was called. The thing he had feared most had finally happened. It came almost as a relief. Based on seeing other prisoners being led away, never to be seen again, he didn't think it was just another interrogation session. He and some other prisoners were led to the gate. The gate guards opened the gates and told them to go. Hesitant the prisoners looked at each other. What was going on? If they walked out of the gate, would they be accused of fleeing and be shot? In no uncertain terms the soldiers told them to go, so they started walking. "Any moment now, I'll get a bullet in my back", Jacobus thought. "Either way, however this may end, I'll be out of here". He kept walking and walking and walking. Long after they were out of range, they sat down to rest. They couldn't believe their good fortune. They all had the same thought: HOME!!

Home for Jacobus was Spaarndam and Agatha, but how to get there? No money, riddled with lice and scabies, emaciated and weak, he knew he couldn't walk there. He remembered Agatha had an aunt and uncle in Soest. Sheer willpower, determination and a friendly man who gave him a ride on the back of his bike got him to the aunt and uncle's house. He had never met these people. How could he expect help from them when they had so little themselves? After he explained who he was and where he came from, they welcomed him with open arms. Symbolically, that is. Physically, he kept his distance and explained he was infested with lice. They dragged a washtub out to the shed and brought him a bar of soap they had saved for a special occasion. They used precious wood to build a fire and burn his prison suit. They gave him clean clothes to wear, a clean bed to sleep in and shared their food with him. Slowly, he started to recover from his ordeal and felt his strength returning, but he was eager to get to Spaarndam where he hoped Agatha was waiting for him. After several days he couldn't wait anymore. Uncle lent him his bicycle and Aunt packed him some food. After thanking the kind and generous couple profusely, he headed direction Spaarndam. He was on his way!

Chapter thirteen

Homecoming

Agatha was sitting at the kitchen table composing a letter to Jacobus's parents. She had not heard from them at all. She hoped they were OK and that they had heard from Jacobus. With rumors of a peace treaty, there were also reports of prisoners being released. Could it really be true? If so, could Jacobus have been released and gone to his parents'? She hoped her letter would reach them and they would send a response. There was a knock on the kitchen window. She looked up and saw an emaciated man in a hat and clothes she didn't recognize. "Agatha", he called, "it's me". She flew up from her chair to open the kitchen door and stumbled over her skirt. She had lost so much weight, her skirt had just fallen from her hips and puddled around her ankles. She paid no attention to it, she ripped the door open and fell into Jacobus's arms. She started sobbing and could not stop. If Jacobus had

had any doubts about finding Agatha waiting for him, they vanished. As he embraced her and tried to comfort her, he knew he was wanted.

Spaarndam had never had a newspaper or newsletter. There was no need. News had a way of finding its way through the community. After five years of hardships, losses and bad news, the good news of Jacobus's release from the concentration camp spread like wildfire. Soon, one after the other, the villagers came to welcome him back. They didn't have much to give, but most didn't come empty handed. One brought an egg "to build you up again". Another brought two potatoes and so it went. They knew how much these small gifts meant, and accepted them gratefully.

Of course, after the excitement died down, Agatha finished her letter to Jacobus's parents and mailed it off, in the hope that they would receive the good news.

After a couple of days of food and rest, the food supply dwindled and Jacobus ventured out on his bicycle. He visited nearby farms and explained that he had just returned from the concentration camp in Amersfoort. Farmers took one look at his bald head, skin marked by louse bites, emaciated body and opened their hearts and larders. Everyday he returned from these trips with eggs, milk, potatoes and whatever else the farmers could spare. It was heartwarming to see the compassion and generosity in the community.

Chapter fourteen

Liberation day

On the fifth of May 1945, Jacobus had only been back a few short weeks, their neighbor came banging on the door, "Have you heard?" "It's over, it's finally over. "The peace treaty has been signed." "Germany has surrendered." Unable to believe the news, Jacobus and Agatha rowed out to the little island in the river where Jacobus's friend had a radio hidden. Yes, it was still there. Somehow he got it to work. Although crackling and noisy, they could understand enough of the broadcast to know it was true. Germany had surrendered! As quickly as they could, they rowed back across the river to share the good news with the rest of the family. It was still hard to believe. After five long years was it really over? They were in the house, relaying what they'd heard on Radio Orange and the BBC, when they heard music coming from outside. Curious, they walked out the door. Some of the houses had the Dutch flag flying: The familiar red, white and blue stripes had not been seen in years. Where had people been hiding them? The sound of music grew louder. Around the bend came the Spaarndam marching band. They had not played or even practiced in five years, but had impromptu assembled when they'd heard the news. Some members were missing. Some still had uniforms or partial uniforms, some didn't. The uniforms bagged around them: everyone had lost so much weight. The music was unrehearsed and off key, but it was unmistakable: The Dutch National Anthem. For the stoic Dutch who pride themselves on the ability to control their emotions, this was too much. People had tears streaming down their faces and with shaky voices, choked with emotion, they attempted to sing along the old familiar text: Wilhelmus van Nassauen, ben ik van Dietse bloed. Het vaderland getrouwe blijf ik tot in den doet. (I am of Dutch blood and will be true to my fatherland until my death). Agatha looked at the band members' familiar faces, now sunken and hollow, and was reminded of the many happy festivities of the past. It seemed like another life. Would things ever be the same again?

A neighbor had a camera and was taking pictures. Film had not been available for years, but he had saved a roll just for this day!

The next day Agatha, still in an elated mood, came downstairs to fix breakfast when she had a reality check. Germany had surrendered, the war was over but there still was no food. What was she going to feed her family? Jacobus tried to console her, "It'll be all right, you'll see, we will get some food". Agatha, who was not at all religious, countered somewhat sarcastically, "Yes, how do you suppose, like manna from heaven?"

They shared what little food they still had and that was that. Jacobus promised he'd go out in the rowboat and try to catch some fish, or maybe visit some of the farms again where he'd been given food before. They were still deliberating the best course of action when they heard the drone of approaching aircraft. Jacobus ran outside to see what was going on and reported back, "Low flying bombers, a whole slew of them." They looked at each other fearfully. They all thought the same thing, "A new invasion? Have the Germans regrouped and are reneging on the peace treaty? Was it all a hoax?" The women took cover under the stairs. Jacobus had gone back out again. He watched as the planes flew over the village. They were flying low and slow and he could easily distinguish star symbols on the wings and then he knew. He ran back inside. "They are American planes" he hollered, "It's all right! They are our allies!" Above a field just outside Spaarndam he saw one of the plane's bomb bay open up and release its load. Some of the other villagers screamed "BOMBS!" and ran for cover. Jacobus felt as if he was nailed to the ground. He simply couldn't believe they were being bombed again. All of a sudden a parachute opened and another and another. "They're not bombs" he hollered. The women came out of the house and together they watched as the parachutes descended. They dared to walk towards the field. As they came closer, they saw barrel like containers on each parachute. With a thud they landed one after another. They waited............no explosions. Puzzled they looked at each other: What could this possibly be? Some of the braver villagers ran to the field to check it out. One of the barrels had burst open upon impact. They couldn't believe their eyes. "It's food" they yelled, "it's really food!"

The town elders immediately organized a distribution system so that everyone would get their fair share. Every person received a loaf of bread, a package of margarine and some milk powder. That night the family had a feast. For the first time in years they could eat their fill. Bread, margarine and milk had never tasted so good. Jacobus looked across the table at Agatha and said, "Did you say something about manna from heaven earlier?" They all laughed. They finally dared to believe that it was over. They were free!!

The food droppings continued until normal supply lines via ship and train were re-established.

Fast forward to 1970. My (American) husband and I had only been married a few weeks when my parents came for a visit. We were living in Germany where my husband was stationed with the Air Force. We did most of our shopping at the commissary on base. My mother offered to help prepare food. When she opened my kitchen cabinet she got all excited. She ran to the living room to get my father. The men came running into the kitchen to see what was the matter. Mom pointed to the open cabinet. Dad got just as excited. Together they emptied my cabinet of the American brand foods they had not seen since 1945. "Oh, look at this: Quaker's Oats, we got those after the war. Oh, and here, Del Monte peaches, remember those? Graham Crackers, oh my gosh!" Having heard the report about the food droppings (every 5th of May when we celebrated liberation day) I understood their excitement and had tears in my eyes watching them re-live the joy of that day so many years ago.

Chapter fifteen

Aftermath

Things were changing rapidly in the Netherlands: The German occupying forces left and Allied Forces took their place. The hated swastika flags were taken down and replaced with the Dutch red, white and blue. The Dutch Royal Family, exiled for five years, returned. A Dutch government was formed and faced the huge task of getting the ravaged country back on its feet. Roads and bridges needed to be rebuilt and repaired, damaged train tracks replaced. Gradually, things improved. Gas and electricity became available again. At first just one or two hours a day, gradually increasing. Lena had two sisters and a brother who had emigrated to the U.S. in the thirties. For five years they had not been able to stay in touch. As soon as international mail was re-established, Lena sent off a long letter to bring her siblings up to date on everything that had happened. How Pieter had suffered before his death and how she'd had to take in her parents. She told them how Opa had become demented before he had passed away, but that Opoe and the rest of the family were alive and well, in spite of all the oppression, hunger, cold and shortages they had endured. As soon as the US family members received the letter, they responded with care packages. Boxes with clothing, shoes, soap, toothpaste and toothbrushes started arriving in Spaarndam. The packages from the U.S. continued to come for several years. Not only did the aunts and uncle donate clothing, their American friends and neighbors started dropping things off for the family members in the Netherlands. Even though the war was over, everything, including food continued to be rationed. The food rations were more plentiful now and nobody was hungry anymore, but it was very basic. One of the care packages contained a box of chocolates: what a treat! Nobody had seen chocolate in a long time. It was a time of joy and hope for the future. Weddings started happening. All the young couples who had met before or during the war and had not wanted to get married under those adverse circumstances, were taking the plunge now. Jacobus and Agatha also wanted to get married. They had waited long enough! How could they though, without a job, money or a place to live? Jacobus had been a successful realtor before the war and he'd had quite a bit of savings, but that was all gone, most of it on black market food during the war. Housing was scarce. So many houses had been destroyed. A new government bureau was established tasked with finding housing for displaced people. Thousands of Dutch returned to the Netherlands from concentration camps and from the Dutch East Indies (now Indonesia). Jacobus found a position with this new bureau. His salary wasn't much, but it was a start.

To combat the housing shortage, people with extra rooms in their house were required to take in lodgers or tenants. If they didn't find tenants themselves, they would be appointed some. This of course resulted in "Rooms for Rent" ads. Agatha found two rooms and a bathroom for rent. Her clever cousin built a drop down kitchen counter over the bathtub and so the bathroom doubled as a kitchen. They were overjoyed: They had a place to live and a job, now they still needed some furnishings. Now that food was more plentiful, it was no longer a valuable method of payment. The new currency was cigarettes! The American soldiers were the only ones who had those. Jacobus came up with a plan to buy furniture, but he needed seed capital. He suggested that Agatha and Dinah would go and chit chat with the American soldiers who were temporarily housed in the Spaarndam school building. Neither one of them spoke much English but he taught them how to say: "Oh, I'm dying for a cigarette!" The plan worked. They came back with a few cigarettes each. Jacobus took these to several farmers in the area and was able to exchange fresh eggs for the cigarettes. He took the eggs to the American soldiers who were tired of eating powdered eggs and gladly exchanged the eggs for more cigarettes. He repeated these transactions several times until he had enough cigarettes to pay for some furniture.

On the 28th of August 1945 Jacobus and Agatha got married. It was a small wedding in the Haarlem town hall. Agatha had sewed an elegant two-piece suit out of her father's pin striped Sunday suit. She wore her wedding shoes that she had saved for five years for this special occasion, except for the trip to Amersfoort. After the ceremony the wedding party returned to Spaarndam, where an aunt had prepared a simple luncheon. Afterwards they bicycled, side by side, to their apartment in Haarlem and their new life – together!

Epilogue

Jacobus and Agatha raised five children and had eight grandchildren. They were married until Jacobus's death at age 85 in 2001. Agatha passed away at age 81 in 2005.

Glossary of Dutch words

Bakfiets – Dutch cargo bike

Duikers – Divers

Honger – Hunger

Onder – Under

Onderduiker – Person in hiding

Opa – Grandpa

Opoe or Oma – Grandma

Poffertjes – Silver dollar size pancakes

Schat – Treasure or Darling

Scheveningen – Name of coastal town

Schrift – Notebook

Tocht – Journey

Glossary of German words

Aufmachen – Open up

Aufstehen – Get up

Frueh – early

Razzia – House-to-house search

About the Author

Maria N. Simpson was born and raised in the Netherlands. She and her husband lived in Germany, the United Kingdom, California, Colorado and Florida.

She is a retired flight attendant and is presently living in Virginia.

Read on for an excerpt of Maria's next book

'FLYING DUTCH WOMAN'

11 September 2001

It was 7AM local time (1Am EST) when I was making my way through the airport to the lower level train station. I was exhausted after working an 8hr flight from Dulles

Airport, VA to Schiphol Airport, Amsterdam, Netherlands. Pushing and pulling heavy carts up and down aisles, serving meals and drinks was hard work. My sister Kiki always joked that I walked across the ocean from the US to Europe. True, for eight hours straight I had been on my feet. For a moment I considered boarding the crew bus with the rest of the crew and go to our hotel and to bed. However, I wanted to see my parents and my sisters. Kiki and I had plans for a little shopping and of course spend some time with her little ones. Three train rides and a taxi cab later I arrived at my parents' house. After breakfast I took a nap, then had some coffee and lunch before Kiki came to pick me up. We parked her car in her driveway, put the baby in the stroller and walked to Main Street where my favorite dress shop had a sale. When crossing the market square Jan, Kiki's husband came running out of his office. He had been trying to call the house, but when he saw us, he came to tell us the alarming news about an attack on the Twin Towers. Impatient to get on with our plans, I told him that had happened before and we'd hear all about it on the news later. We pressed on to the dress shop, but my heart wasn't really in it as I started to process Jan's words. I suggested we'd stop by the bank where I needed some local currency from the ATM and go home and turn on the TV. The ATM machine refused to spit out the necessary cash while the display showed that no satellite connection to the US was available. That did it! Now I got really worried. We walked back and turned on the TV while the phone started ringing. It was my sister Leny who had been trying to reach us. I watched in horror while Leny filled me in about what had happened. When I heard about the United and American Airlines planes that had flown into the towers, filled with my colleagues, I lost it. Then came the news that United flight 93 was lost and unaccounted for. I was sobbing at that point. Kiki put her arms around me and said, crying, "Maybe you should give up this dangerous job". "What else should I do", I asked. "Work in a nice, safe office like I do" was her answer." Like all the people that went to work in their nice, safe offices in the Twin Towers this morning?" I asked in response. A short time later came the report that the missing flight 93 had crashed in PA. My hopes that that plane had been OK were dashed. Stunned, I watched as the reports went on and on: The Pentagon had been hit, that was close to home. I tried to call my husband and my daughter in VA. All phone connections to the States were down. I called the purser in the hotel. She had been unable to contact United Airlines. Normally, the United Airlines crew desk could be reached on a toll-free line from anywhere in the world. The system was now unavailable. We were cut off from communicating with our company. What about the scheduled flight back the following day? The TV reported that all US Airports had closed. We knew we weren't going home the next day. When would we be able to?

Right after I had left my parents' house, their phone started ringing off the hook. Friends and family members who all knew that I worked for United Airlines called to inquire if my parents had heard from me. Normally, my parents never knew where or when I was flying. I was on reserve and at a moment's notice I would be on my way to the airport with an assignment to anywhere USA or Europe. Thankfully, this time they knew exactly where I was and so did my husband back home. I had left him a note with my flight numbers and destination. My daughter Carla who lives in Germany called Kiki to ask if maybe she had heard from me. Like me, Carla had not been able to get through to her father or her sister. She was relieved to hear that I was safe. I realized I should have called her but I hadn't been thinking clearly.

The following days I spent in a daze riveted to the TV. I switched from British to Dutch to German channels and to CNN. Kiki and Jan went to work, the children to kindergarten and daycare. I seemed to be unable to do anything but watch the news. The death toll kept rising. My heart broke for all the people that lost loved ones. I watched with tears in my eyes as people posted pictures of family members and friends that were unaccounted for.

Of course, I had not been prepared to spend more than an overnight. I had to borrow some money to buy some clothing and other needed articles. Kiki's family physician went through a great deal of trouble to provide me with the medications I required and had only brought a two-day supply. I was never charged by either the doctor or the pharmacy. Everybody went out of their way to be helpful. My colleagues in the hotel experienced nothing but kindness and helpfulness. Not knowing how long the crew was going to be there, unable to contact United, the hotel not only let them stay there, but lent them money and gave them free meals. A friendly soul took a group of them on a sightseeing tour in his van, just to take their minds of things for a little while.

The Dutch government decided to have a few minutes of silence to honor the victims of the attack. From the house I could see all traffic on the interstate come to a full stop at the designated time. The compassion and care shown by my country of birth felt like a warm embrace.

The Dutch TV station published the lists of passengers and crew members perished on the four planes. In stunned silence I recognized Ceecee's name on the crew downed in PA. I had met Ceecee on my commuter flight to Miami when I still lived in Florida. We both stood by for space available to get home. We ended up seated next to each other and shared a few laughs. We kept bumping into each other on our flights to and from Miami. She had been a police officer, but quit and became a flight attendant when her husband found her job as a police officer in Miami too dangerous.

During my daily phone call to the purser I was told that the sister of one of my fellow crewmembers had also been on that fated flight 93.

After a week United finally was able to make contact with the purser. We were to work our return flight the following day. The captain conducted a briefing on the plane before the passengers boarded. There was a new rule: Nobody had access to the cockpit anymore. If we needed to enter the flight deck, we were to call first. We were given a code word to use if there was a threat. Our training until then had been to give in to hijacker's demands. The goal was to save as many lives as possible. The events of 9/11 changed everything. The cockpit was bolted from the inside. Access was only granted after calling with the "all clear" code and after all passengers in the front were seated. There were no more casual visits to the flight deck to have a chat with the pilots who were bored during long flights.

We expressed our concern about the middle easterners we had seen in the boarding area. The captain has the authority to deny boarding to any passenger if he feels it is necessary. He refused to exercise his right. "I will not do to them what was done to our Japanese citizens during WWII" he said. We, as cabin crew had the right to refuse to fly if we feared for our lives. We looked at each other, we all wanted to get home to our families.

I cannot adequately describe the atmosphere on that return flight. The tension was palpable. We kept an eye on the middle eastern passengers at all times.

At Dulles we were met by a United welcoming committee. We all shed some tears.

The drive home from the airport took much longer than usual. I had been unable to contact my husband for the entire week. He did not know I was on my way home. My cell phone was empty and I had not wanted to take time to charge it at the airport. He must have been on the lookout, though. As soon as I pulled into the garage he came running out of the house. Crying, we fell into each other's arms.

Later we heard about friends' and family's experiences. A friend narrowly escaped death at the Pentagon. Fellow flight attendants got stranded at various places around the world. I had been lucky. I could have been stranded anywhere, instead I had been with friends and family.